The Last Years of Stean

EASTERN REGION

PAUL LEAVENS & SVMRC

Copyright Book Law Publications – First published in the United Kingdom in 2019

ISBN 978-1-909625-95-2

Printed and bound by The Amadeus Press, Cleckheaton, West Yorkshire

Published by Book Law Publications, 382 Carlton Hill, Nottingham, NG4 1JA

Introduction

This album was created from illustrations emanating from two sources: The camera of Paul Leavens – PL/BLP – and the collection of the Sour Valley Model Railway Club – SVMRC. Most, if not all, of the images have never been published and hopefully will be seen as a refreshing look at the final days of steam on the old Eastern Region mainly from 1959 to 1963.

Our starting point is Doncaster, about as far north that the Eastern Region got before it petered out to a couple of running lines where it bordered the North Eastern Region near Selby. From Doncaster we head south but not entirely in a straight line. We have used the East Coast Main Line – ECML – as a datum point and as we proceed southwards we deviate right and left, west and east, to look at centres away from the main line but which had plenty to offer enthusiasts at the time. Sheffield during early BR days was covered by two regions the ER and London Midland Region which though inter-connected geographically were miles apart in other regards. It was a situation which enthusiasts endured but one which BR had to change to bring under a single management team – the ER – which they did from 1958. From Sheffield we make our way east to Retford where that flat crossing caused so much delay. Off then to Lincoln to follow one of the regular diversion routes. Heading back west we meet the ECML at Peterborough where another mecca of steam was created by numerous companies coming together and where each had their own piece of turf. Next is Cambridge followed by Colchester which for this album is as far as we go in an easterly direction as we get. Regaining the ECML at Hatfield, we then make our way into the suburbs of North London before reaching the terminus at King's Cross.

On the way we have met numerous classes of steam and a few diesel locomotives, some many times with those ER Pacifics dominating some of the geography. We go lineside, aloft, and onto the station platforms to bring some stunning views of well-known places and some less so.

It has been a pleasure putting this album together the only downside was what do we leave out? However, we could always revisit those areas again in a future album. Just say the word!

David Allen, Newstead Abbey, Nottinghamshire, January 2019.

(*front cover*) Top Shed towards the end in 1963 with A4s – what else – Nos.60007 and 60017. *PL/BLP.*

(*rear cover, top*) Up express departs Grantham with V2 No.60871 in charge on 25th September 1960. *PL/BLP.*

(*rear cover, bottom*) Down express with A3 No.60102 at Wood Green 9th September 1960. *PL/BLP.*

DONCASTER

(*above*) This is Doncaster home of the 'Plant' locomotive works and birthplace of Gresley's wonderful Pacifics. On this superb Tuesday morning of 4th August 1959 two Peppercorn engines, A1 No.60150 WILLBROOK and K1 No.62057, are being hauled towards the works for attention by an unidentified O4/8. The Pacific is about to undergo a six-week long General overhaul which will put it back into traffic on 17th September whereas the 2-6-0 is entering for a Casual Light repair which didn't require the tender being emptied. This view was captured from St James' bridge located just south of the Central passenger station and the vantage point for many of the illustrations presented herein. *SVMRC.*

(*below*) Leaving the engine shed and yards at Doncaster Carr behind, one of Copley Hill's Peppercorn A1s, No.60141 ABBOTSFORD runs towards Doncaster station with the Down *YORKSHIRE PULLMAN* on a summers' evening in 1961. *SVMRC.*

(*above*) Right behind the Pullman came Doncaster based Thompson B1 No.61326 with eight Gresley bogies showing an express headcode and the number 13 on what appears to be a special board. *SVMRC*.

(*below*) Just after midday on an overcast summers day in 1960, A4 No.60032 GANNET heads north through Doncaster station with the Down service of *THE ELIZABETHAN* to the delight of the 'spotters' on platform No.5. King's Cross shed have done their usual magnificent cleaning job on the Pacific which was one of the select band of regular engines used on this prestige express. Note the Deltic prototype on the Down side. *SVMRC*.

(*above*) Wearing those distinctive smoke deflectors, King's Cross A3 No.60109 HERMIT takes the Up fast line through Doncaster with an express during the summer of 1961. Note the reversed headboard placed on the upper lamp iron; this method of returning the headboards' to their point of origin was a favoured way of transporting the boards which allayed the possibility of damage if carried in the locomotive cabs. Dairycoates K3 No.61871 awaits a signal at the Down platform end and would have been there for a service from Sheffield which it would take over for the run to Hull. *SVMRC.*

(*below*) Hull Dairycoates D49 No.62765 THE GOATHLAND sneaking into platform No.1 with a train – looks like a Pullman set – from Hull in August 1960. *SVMRC.*

Copley Hill's Peppercorn A1 No.60120 KITTIWAKE has charge of the Up service of the *YORKSHIRE PULLMAN* this morning and is making its way out of Doncaster gingerly – the last few Pullman cars are just being drawn onto the Up main-line so let's not spill any coffee – and with 156 miles before journey's end there would be plenty of opportunity to open up the big Pacific. Note the platelayers going about their work checking the gauge of the Down main. *SVMRC.*

(*above*) Having brought the main train – which included in the formation a portion from Bradford and one from Harrogate – from Leeds, the A1 uncoupled, drew forward, reversed into platform No.1, collects the Hull portion draws forward onto the Up main, and then reverses the four vehicles back to the waiting train standing in platform No.4. Once the formation is assembled the *YORKSHIRE PULLMAN* with its West and East Riding business types would set off for King's Cross as depicted opposite. The process took place every weekday morning. *SVMRC*.

(*below*) A few minutes later, we cross the road and look over the parapet of the south wall of the bridge and spot Grantham A3 No.60106 FLYING FOX bringing a Down express into the busy precincts of Doncaster station. A mineral train hauled by Doncaster based O4/8 No.63858 has managed to get a path behind the Pullman but the crew of that train would have to work smartly in order to clear the Up main before the next express appears from the north. *SVMRC*.

A3 No.60106 runs to Doncaster Carr engine shed for servicing prior to returning home. The atrocious state of the locomotive was typical of the period but there is some nice tender detail to be had for all those modellers. *SVMRC*.

A Newcastle-Colchester express headed by York based B16/3 No.61463 heads south along the Up slow. The 4-6-0 would have taken over the hefty looking train at York, relieving a Gateshead V2 or whatever was available this morning. The track men are out in force on this rather sunny morning and the measuring team have moved on a few yards to the next set of points. *SVMRC*.

(*above*) Backwards and forwards across St James' bridge and ever mindful of the road traffic, we now look south again and are greeted by six steam locomotives in view. Amongst their lot is the 9F No.92162, four K3s in the carriage sidings, and 36A based Peppercorn A1 No.60114 W.P.ALLEN proceeding along the Down main from the shed. All trains using the Down slow here had to stop to use the Down fast line to clear the station throat at this south end where the line from Sheffield and points west joined the ECML. *SVMRC*.

(*below*) A1 No.60158 ABERDONIAN runs beneath our vantage point hauling a Hull-King's Cross express. The popularity of the bridge is obvious from this aspect and some of the younger element tended to really 'chance it!' perching on the parapet. *SVMRC*.

(*above*) As the Peppercorn Pacific strides out a Gresley O2 approaches from the south with a train of mainly mineral empties. Another resident of these parts, No.63941 wears the uniform of the practically uncared-for. Perhaps a transfer to Grantham in November 1961 would see the 2-8-0 get a bit more attention from the cleaners but that shed, like all the others, was bereft of personnel for cleaning engines. However, let's look at another aspect of railways in this area. On the right footplate abreast the smokebox stands what initially appears to be a milk churn but it was in fact a similar vessel made to carry water. That no doubt was bound for one of the isolated signal boxes found virtually everywhere which were not connected to any water supply and so had to be supplied by the next locomotive to go that way. *SVMRC.*

(*below*) Peppercorn A1 No.60144 KING'S COURIER, one of Doncaster's own, approaches St James' bridge in 1959 with thirteen on; the nearest vehicles are articulated twins which were once part of the pre-war *CORONATION* train set but since used as ordinary passenger stock and found in numerous formations on the ECML. A diesel shunter is working the yard on the Up side of the main line. *SVMRC.*

Heading towards Sheffield via the SYR line, K3 No.61845 has charge of a short afternoon passenger working during what appears to be a quiet time at Doncaster. The Lincoln based 2-6-0 features again in this Doncaster sequence later on. Note the Up side main-line pilot waiting patiently for any misbehaving locomotives; that particular duty disappeared after May 1964. *SVMRC*.

On one of its last outings before it was condemned, Thompson B1 No.61033 DIBATAG from Canklow makes its way home with a freight train on a superb afternoon in March 1963 watched by the spotters on St James' bridge. *SVMRC*.

Back to the station to watch the fireman on the tender of A2/3 No.60520 OWEN TUDOR wrestling with the bag and the column arm to get a refill of water from the Up side mid-platform column just as Heaton A3 No.60083 SIR HUGO runs through with an Up express from Newcastle in 1960. *SVMRC*.

After completing a General overhaul, Haymarket A3 No.60098 SPION KOP is prepared for a revenue earning run which would take it some way towards home on Friday 26th May 1961. The stock is still being 'fettled' by the yard staff at Garden sidings. *SVMRC*.

Re-locating to the north end of the station, we get a view of the carriage works at Doncaster although the exhaust from A1 No.60133 POMMERN is hiding the bulk of the resident vehicles awaiting repair or overhaul. *SVMRC.*

Switching from the Up fast to the Up slow, A1 No.60116 HAL O' THE WYND prepares for a station stop at Doncaster in June 1962. Not long off Doncaster 'Plant' works, the Pacific had just undergone its final overhaul – 26th April to 2nd June 1962 – a General which would see it through to its June 1965 condemnation. The coal in the tender is not exactly the best available in these parts. Now that background formed by the carriage works and the various sidings and assorted stock makes a pleasing sight not quite available today. *SVMRC.*

Just a few weeks old, EE Type 4 D392 hogs the Down main at Doncaster in June 1962 whilst hauling the non-stop *ANGLO SCOTTISH CAR CARRIER*. Alongside another Down service composed of ex-LMS coaches gets underway from the station but is soon overtaken by the northbound Holloway-Stirling express. The diesel would only experience a few more months of this main-line express passenger haulage because it was transferred from Gateshead to Thornaby where freight was the bread-and-butter for the allocation there. *SVMRC*.

One of the positive spin-offs from the BR 1955 Modernisation Plan was the fact that diesel locomotives from other regions, sometimes many hundreds of miles away, would regularly appear on your local lines hauling trains which had also originated on other regions. One of the regular – daily – appearances on the ECML as far north as York, was the SR Type 3 diesel-electrics which usually double-headed the heavy Cliffe-Uddingston cement hopper trains. This image from June 1962 shows a pair of the BRC&W Bo-Bo Type 3s – D6582 and an unidentified sister working home to the Southern Region with a train of empty hoppers over the Up fast at Doncaster. *SVMRC*.

(*above*) V2 No.60948 runs along the Down main in June 1961 with a northbound express during another quiet spell although away from the main line the diesel shunters are busy. The March based V2 was soon to return to the ECML sheds with New England, Grantham and Doncaster using its services before it was condemned at Doncaster on 22nd September 1963. Before then though it would enter Doncaster 'Plant' works for a General overhaul when separate cylinders would be fitted. *SVMRC*.

(*below*) With a WD 2-8-0 coming along the Up main with a mineral train, Doncaster based B1 No.61270 heads south with a rather mixed freight during a lull in passenger traffic in summer 1961. *SVMRC*.

And here she comes! The Deltic prototype – in all her glory – glides into platform No.8 at Doncaster in August 1960 with a Down express. The English Electric diesel was placed at the mercy of BR to do what they would with it and on the Eastern Region she was put into service alongside the region's numerous Pacifics for evaluate. Eventually BR placed an order for twenty-two of the 3,300 h.p. diesel-electrics but they were destined for the ER-NER-ScR ECML traffic only. The LMR had gone for electrification of the WCML; the WR had gone for diesel-hydraulics whilst the SR had only required a small fleet of diesel locomotives to satisfy their needs as electric-multiple units became their principal people movers. *SVMRC.*

Another rarity around these parts for most of the time Haymarket A3 No.60043 BROWN JACK runs north through platform No.8 almost unnoticed as soon as the Deltic had departed. The Pacific had just finished works trials after a General overhaul – 27th June to 5th August 1960 – and was now proceeding homewards having topped up its coal bunker at Carr shed. *SVMRC*

You could have thought that a competition was afoot to produce the dirtiest locomotive running on BR but there was no competition and if there was everyone would be a winner! B1 No.61272 from New England sets off from Doncaster with a Down express during the summer of 1961 as the Down service of *THE FLYING SCOTSMAN* thunders through the station on the Down main behind Gateshead based EE Type 4 D239. *SVMRC*.

This is what they looked like when ex-works – brand new! As it passes the carriage works offices facing platform 8 at Doncaster station, K3 No.61845 carries the lamp on the centre lower lamp-iron signifying it is on Doncaster works trials. The 2-6-0 was allocated to March at this date, just after its summer 1960 and last incidentally, General overhaul – 7th July to 11th August 1960. It would transfer to Colwick in December 1960 and then Lincoln three months later. *SVMRC*.

(*above*) O4 No.63902 rumbles through Doncaster during a lull in the morning parade of express passenger trains in late summer 1960. The main station was given the name Doncaster (Central) in 1923 but in 1951 Central was dropped and it became the only station in the town used for the public. St James' Bridge station was closed in 1946 but it had never been a whole-time station and was only used for race meeting, the Great Central having opened their route to London saw fit to open a Doncaster station which brought excursions from all over their system. It became St James' Bridge at the Grouping to distinguish the two stations. *SVMRC.*

(*below*) Relegation came in many forms! York A2/3 No.60516 HYCILLA, a recent unwanted acquisition from Heaton – 12th June – is working a northbound freight back home in August 1960. The Thompson Pacific would actually come back to Doncaster in the following January for a major overhaul which would prove to be its last. It was condemned in November 1962 and returned to Doncaster one last time – for cutting! *SVMRC.*

(*above*) Another one for the 'Plant' works! WD 2-8-0 No.90636, one of 36A's own, drags a dead Peppercorn K1 from Carr shed to the locomotive works for attention on 26th May 1961. The 2-6-0 is unidentified but it would have been down for overhaul rather than the chop. A3 No.60098 is still waiting in Garden sidings with its train. Meanwhile on the platform at St James' Bridge station the spotters numbers are building, the promised sunshine bringing them from far and wide. It will be another good day methinks! *SVMRC.*

(*below*) Back at Doncaster station A4 No.60015 QUICKSILVER runs into platform No.8 with a Down express in August 1961. The station modernisation proceeds and all the new lamps are now in situ. The throng of 'spotters' take stock of the 'Streak' as it seemingly glides effortlessly into the platform. The road bridge from which we took so many of the previous illustrations stands in the background like a sentinel guarding the approaches. *SVMRC.*

(*above*) It was getting busy again, at least with non-stoppers. Like an old friend, A4 No.60026 MILES BEEVOR is greeted or otherwise by the 'spotters' who are now not just inhabiting the platforms ends, they are spreading out along the platform mingling with the passengers and to some causing a nuisance. The tolerance of the staff was wearing thin! Meanwhile the canopies over each platform have been transformed from the overall roof which once covered this area. *SVMRC.*

(*below*) The spotters' nightmare taking place! A non-stop express with a 'Streak' – the driver did whistle as he came under the bridge to the north of the station – rushes through at the maximum permitted speed whilst two trains hog the inner platforms Nos.4 and 5. It is now that the benefit of the platform end location is appreciated! A4 No.60008 DWIGHT D. EISENHOWER heads the non-stop. *SVMRC.*

(*above*) Meanwhile on the Down main A4 No.60027 MERLIN runs through with *THE ELIZABETHAN* on its non-stop journey to Edinburgh (Waverley). The track layout here can be appreciated even with an express passing through. SVMRC.

(*below*) An afternoon Hull (Paragon)-Liverpool (Central) express rolls into platform No.1 during September 1959 with Darnall B1 No.61139 doing the honours as far as Sheffield (Victoria) where electric haulage would take over. The B1 was a new arrival at Darnall shed during the previous June having spent the last twelve years working from sheds at the southern end of the ECML. Having had a chance to stretch its legs on the journey over the flatlands from Hull, the 4-6-0 will have numerous junctions and speed restrictions to contend with on the final section of its involvement with the train. The Hull-Liverpool service over the former GCR via Manchester (Central) and the Cheshire Lines used to generate a train each way every couple of hours in steam days. And if that route didn't appeal you could use the former L&NWR line from Liverpool (Lime Street) via Manchester (Exchange), Standedge tunnel and Leeds. That's right the ex-L&YR line from Liverpool (Exchange) via Wigan, Manchester (Victoria), Summit tunnel, Halifax, Bradford and Leeds was another possibility. All three routes appeared well patronised as witness this gathering at Doncaster. Note also the parcels traffic! *SVMRC*.

Class leader No.60800 GREEN ARROW heads south beneath St James' bridge whilst WD 2-8-0 No.90482 heads north to collect a train. *SVMRC.*

Another V2! With a truly mixed bag of stock in tow, New England's No.60853 sets out for the north with twelve on circa 1959. Once the train clears Marshgate Junction – behind the photographer – the falling gradient changes to eight miles of level running before a small roller-coaster of short gradients is encountered – no problem for this engine. *SVMRC.*

THE LAST YEARS OF STEAM ON THE EASTERN REGION

(*above*) Thompson's truly grotesque alteration of Gresley A1 Pacific No.4470 GREAT NORTHERN into the A1/1 was a step too far for many. However, the Pacific carried on in service for another seventeen years and here during its final year No.60113 is heading south with a fitted freight. Except for the shunter over on the works sidings, Doncaster is quiet once again. *SVMRC*.

(*below*) With an express from Newcastle (Central) to the Capital in August 1961, Heaton based A3 No.60072 SUNSTAR in a deplorable external state runs along the Up fast past Garden Sidings and the southern junction giving access to the former South Yorkshire Railway lines; the signal box was Bridge Junction. This view point at the Balby Road bridge completes the trio of excellent vantage points available to photographers around Doncaster station, not to mention the footbridge spanning Central station too. It is from here we use the SYR to give us a route to Sheffield where the Eastern Region has just expanded its territory to include the old Midland lines. *SVMRC*.

SHEFFIELD & Environs

(*above*) It might be former Midland Railway territory but Rotherham (Masborough) station was now well inside the Eastern Region. To gain the LMR you would now have to proceed west across the Pennines or journey south into Derbyshire. To complicate matters, 8F No.48070 was from the North Eastern Region at Royston shed which was not too far away from here and was one of the main sources of freight motive power on this line which served heavy industry, and numerous coal mines. Photographed during a sunny morning in 1960, this station no longer exists and has been replaced by a more centralised establishment – Rotherham (Central) – built to the north and east of this station. *SVMRC.*

(*below*) Seen from the platform of the erstwhile Broughton Lane station in June 1959, Thompson B1 No.61316 heads a Hull-Liverpool express round the curve past the continuous pilot coal stage associated with the goods yard to the north on the west side. The creation of Tinsley marshalling yard on the land in the right background would see the likes of Broughton Lane closed. The Darnall engine was between works visit hence its atrocious external condition. The station here was part of the MS&LR empire and was opened in August 1864; it closed on 3rd April 1956, unusually, a Tuesday because Monday 2nd April was a Bank Holiday! *SVMRC.*

(*above*) D11 'Director' No.62666 ZEEBRUGGE departs from platform No.4 at Victoria station in 1959 with an express for Cleethorpes; the train originating in Manchester. Resident now at Sheffield Darnall shed, this 4-4-0 had literally been allocated to nearly every ex-GC engine shed on the system besides one or two others of GNR origin. 1959 would prove to be the penultimate year when this engine has work but most of that would be seasonal with long periods in store. Nevertheless, the D11 was still a capable class but evolution was continuously overtaking them and work was fast disappearing. Only this particular job with its sea-side destination became regular along with semi-fasts and all-stations to Nottingham after which it was storage. No.62666 was sent into Doncaster works for cutting up on the day it was condemned. *SVMRC*.

(*below*) Colwick K3 No.61914 departs from Victoria in the summer of 1958 with *THE SOUTH YORKSHIREMAN*. How far the 2-6-0 would work the express is unknown but Nottingham would appear to be the logical changeover but Leicester had the A3s and the V2s for handling these trains so perhaps that was the aim for the K3? *SVMRC*.

Not an everyday sight at Sheffield Vic but the Peppercorn A1s got there now and again on running-in turns or covering for a rostered B1 or K3. This is No.60125 SCOTTISH UNION in bay platform No.1 during 1958, not long after the Pacific was transferred to Doncaster from King's Cross. Two other east-bound departures appear imminent with Darnall B1 No.61150 – nearest – having just been given the green flag whilst Mexborough's No.61165 blows off impatiently. *SVMRC.*

The A1 gets away. Not long after this image was recorded the Pacific went into works at Doncaster for a General overhaul and a change of emblem to crest on the tender. *SVMRC.*

Having just replaced a MSW EM2 at Sheffield (Victoria), one of Darnall's Thompson B1s, No.61377, deviates from the GC mainline at Woodburn Junction and heads towards Doncaster with a morning working of a Liverpool (Central)-Hull (Paragon) express in September 1960. The five vehicle train is a hotchpotch of coaches but the intending passengers were not bothered as long as they got a seat. Within two years of this image being recorded, the 4-6-0 was condemned at Langwith shed and sold to a Sheffield yard for scrap. In the background, just above the front of the second vehicle is the bridge spanning the former L&NWR lines down to Nunnery where the west coast Company had their Sheffield foot-hold! The two gentlemen in the doorway of the building on the Down side of the main line were employed by the National Coal Board at the former Nunnery Colliery which had closed in 1953 but was still partly in use to pump water from associated workings in the vicinity. *SVMRC*.

Heading a Down working towards Victoria, Retford B1 No.61212 hurries past Darnall depot with the little used electric shed on the right. The Cravens factory complex sprawls away to the east, busy building diesel multiple units at this time for BR besides export orders all over the globe. Those were the days! *SVMRC*.

(*above*) On an unknown date in 1960, K3 No.61922 and another engine obscured by smoke, accelerate past Cravens railway vehicle manufactory on the right, and the Down side entrance to Darnall engine shed on the left. The K3 still wears a 53A shed plate for Dairycoates which was soon to change to 50B. *SVMRC.*

(*below*) Kentish Town 'Scot' No.46123 ROYAL IRISH FUSILIER runs through Attercliffe Road station with an Up express on a superb winters' morning in 1960. Slightly elevated above the surrounding factories and yards, Attercliffe Road was the penultimate station before Sheffield (Midland) coming from the north; it dated from February 1870 when the Midland was entering Sheffield from the Rotherham direction. It appears in this view to have been rebuilt with modern modular concrete platforms. The station closed on 30th January 1995. The 7P was a newcomer to the old LMS Midland Division having spent all of its life up to its September 1959 transfer from Edge Hill to Kentish Town working from Western Division sheds. Just prior to withdrawal it managed to return to its former hunting grounds at Carlisle Upperby. *SVMRC.*

(*above*) With the rear of its inter-regional express train just clearing Attercliffe Road station, Barrow Road 'Jubilee' No.45572 EIRE passes the Council depot just north of Nunnery Junction. The bridge being traversed by the third vehicle was known locally as Norfolk Bridge and spanned the local navigation. During its journey this express will pass from North Eastern Region to ER, to LMR, to Western Region; with the same locomotive throughout and over the former Midland Railway line too all the way to Bristol! *SVMRC*.

(*below*) Above the railway on which No.45572 was heading south, was the former Manchester, Sheffield & Lincolnshire main line now much changed from those pre-GCR days with electric traction taking over from steam between Sheffield and Manchester. This is EM2 No.27006 PANDORA outside the carriage shed located on the Up side of the line east of Victoria station. The big electric locomotive will collect its stock from here for the next westbound working . *SVMRC*.

Back on the old Midland line, we get a glimpse through the tunnels and bridges between Midland station and Nunnery junction. 'Crab' No.42794 approaches with an Up passenger train. *SVMRC.*

'Jubilee' No.45650 BLAKE has charge of the Down service of *THE WAVERLEY* as it exits the tunnels at Nunnery beneath the GC main line in October 1959. The Nottingham based 6P would have taken the train onto Leeds where it terminated at City station and where a 6P, 7P or double-headed combination would have reversed onto the rear of the formation and taken the Anglo-Scottish express on the next stage of its journey to Carlisle. No.45650 would then have been free to proceed to Holbeck shed for servicing. As the ER took on more diesel locomotives in the early 1960s, they were able to send a handful of Gresley A3s to work the Anglo-Scottish expresses over the Settle-Carlisle route. This express was another true inter-regional affair involving LMR, ER, NER, and ScR. Not to mention multiple changes of motive power. If you had the time it was a nice way to travel from London to Edinburgh; a bit of an enthusiasts' ideal journey really. *SVMRC.*

South of Midland station and Canklow 4F No.44576 runs empty stock past the Queens Road goods yard in August 1960. The former Midland roundhouse changed its shed code to 41D from 19C when the Eastern Region took over in 1958. *SVMRC.*

Another 'Scot'! No.46160 QUEEN VICTORIA'S RIFLEMAN accelerates away from Sheffield (Midland) with an express for London (St Pancras) in April 1960. This was another 'Scot' which had been cascaded from the WCML to the Midland Lines of the LMR as more main-line diesels arrived. After twelve years at Longsight, the 7P was transferred to Kentish Town in September 1959. Note the new paintwork around the smokebox, the only sign of a Heavy Intermediate overhaul this engine received just weeks beforehand. The tender still carries the BR emblem which would be replaced during a Heavy General in September 1961 but in the meantime this engine has some serious mileage to cover if it's to break the two-million miles barrier. At the end of the year it was still 60,000 miles shy of the magic number but there were four years and five months to manage that figure. I'd like to think it completed the quest but those latter years were fraught with long periods of redundancy - was 15,000 a year possible? *SVMRC.*

(*above*) Shortly after departure from Sheffield (Midland), Millhouses 'Jubilee' No.45576 BOMBAY gets the southbound *DEVONIAN* on its way to those South Devon resorts which became so popular in post-war Britain. This would be at some time in early 1961. Although the external appearance of the 4-6-0 looks rather bad, its mechanical condition and steaming qualities were fine. If all goes well the 6P would work as far as Bristol where a WR engine would take over for the run through Somerset and Devon. Note the coal looks to be of reasonable quality and nicely stacked. The building on the right with the nice range of chimneys atop a castellated tower was part of the former BR offices located there and known locally as the 'Farm' and which were vacated when Sheaf House was opened adjacent to Midland station. Question time! If this engine had been preserved would it have been politically correct to change its name to MUMBIA? It'll leave that one with you. *SVMRC.*

(*below*) Back on the GC main we come across the Darnall engine shed outlet road on the Down side of the line with one of the crew from Lincoln B1 No.61042 about to telephone his request for release. The adjacent bridge carries the shed inlet road from the Up side. Like the shed itself, all these facilities were provided during WW2 for the depot's opening in 1943 some three years before the Thompson 4-6-0 was built at the NBL Co. in Glasgow. *SVMRC.*

(*above*) Passing an unidentified but new diesel multiple unit car located on the Craven's siding in 1960, green-liveried EM1 No.26020 makes its way to Rotherwood sidings to pick-up a westbound freight. Note the train heating hose dangling beneath the buffer beam signifying that this particular EM1 was equipped to haul passenger stock in winter and for which purpose the locomotive was fitted with a train heating boiler, the only other members of the class so fitted were the final batch 26046 to 26057 – all named – and the pioneer 26000 TOMMY. Note also the height of the wires here which saw the pantographs at virtually full stretch. *SVMRC.*

(*below*) It appears that V2 fans are in for a treat today as everywhere we look a V2 appears from nowhere! This is No.60815 working south – or is that east – through Woodhouse West Junction with a train for Marylebone. It is possibly *THE SOUTH YORKSHIREMAN* but that is pure speculation. But then it could be a Bradford-Bournemouth? The world is your oyster! The vantage point is Furnace Lane bridge and is the first section of the old GC main line east of Sheffield free of the overhead catenary of the MSW electrification. It is also where southbound (Up) trains used to open up and stretch their legs as the V2 is doing here. It is nice to report that the station here is still operational. *SVMRC.*

Working a local turn, J11 No.64373 has plenty of steam as it heads east out of Woodhouse with this taxing load in June 1961. Note the state of the coal in the tender!! *SVMRC.*

Looking east into the morning sun we see the sidings at Woodhouse as a WD 2-8-0 No.90275 of 41J runs west with a short mineral train towards Sheffield. In the distance, where the semaphore signals mark the start of the junction between the original MS&LR route to the east and the new route to the south and London. Note the rather cut-off signal box – Woodhouse Sidings – lay close to the ground. The eagle-eyed would have noticed some new DMUs at the other end of the sidings. These were ex-Cravens whose building works was not far away. *SVMRC.*

THE LAST YEARS OF STEAM ON THE EASTERN REGION

With an eastbound freight, Langwith's O4 No.63833 leaves the catenary behind and runs into open country just west of Woodhouse station in June 1961. *SVMRC.*

Making a bit of a fuss on that June morning in 1961, Dairycoates K3 No.61897 brings a train of empty fish vans – they are supposed to be white-liveried Blue Spot fish vans – through Woodhouse and heads eventually towards Hull via Doncaster. *SVMRC.*

(*above*) Coming the other way in the Up direction that morning was another K3 – No.61919 from Lincoln – which had charge of yet another freight train. It is amazing just how much freight traffic there was on the rails then, even though it was diminishing, and sights such as this were all day, every day in most areas. We've just shown two K3s as at summer 1961, this one would be gone within a year whereas the Hull example lasted until December 1962. *SVMRC.*

(*below*) Having reached Woodhouse, Colwick L1 No.67775 has nearly completed its journey from Nottingham (Victoria) to Sheffield (Victoria) with an all stations early morning stopper consisting two sets of articulated carriages which were regulars on this service, the nearest set with its flush sides is totally alien to this compiler but is willing to know all about if some kind soul could enlighten him. The L1 was a fairly new arrival at Colwick shed having transferred there from Ipswich in March 1960. However, this summer was to be its last and after the summer timetable ended it was condemned and sent to Darlington for scrapping. *SVMRC.*

Nipping round the back at Woodhouse station, O4 No.63912 from Langwith runs south with an Up freight. Looking at the surrounds to this station, it is difficult to realise that we were in the heart of coal mining and coke producing plants, all of which have now gone. *SVMRC*.

With a fitted freight in tow, York based V2 No.60907 starts the transition from Up main to Up slow just after Woodhouse station in 1961. Note the coaling stage and pit – for the one-time continuous pilot – behind the signal box. *SVMRC*.

Deputising for the rostered 'Britannia'? March B1 No.61204 enters unfamiliar territory at Woodhouse in 1960 whilst hauling the Harwich-Liverpool boat train; and running late too. A better view of the sidings can be had now that the haze is clearing. *SVMRC*.

A last look at Woodhouse with Norwich Thorpe 'Britannia' No.70007 COUR-DE-LION approaching with the northbound service of the Harwich (Parkeston Quay)-Liverpool (Central) boat train – also known as the North Country Continental – on another stage of its torturous journey from the east coast to the west coast which in BR days, from 1954 onwards, saw four changes of motive power, two methods of haulage, steam and electric, a reversal, and a myriad of stops en route. With twelve on, the Pacific has not had too easy a job working over from Essex but the real test will come when No.70007 retires to Darnall shed whilst an EM2 takes on the train for the run over Woodhead from Sheffield to Guide Bridge where a Cl.4 2-6-4T will couple onto the train for the run to Manchester (Central) which was mainly downhill anyway. Can the eagle-eyed see those new Cravens DMUs in the sidings? *SVMRC*.

RETFORD

Mexborough B1 No.61194 waits for the signal at Retford which will put it onto the ECML in September 1962. It doesn't look too clever but the B1 was in fine mechanical condition which will help it overcome the misgivings of the contents of the tender. However, whilst awaiting its opportunity to motor south towards New England, the 4-6-0 had a chance to compare the SR Type 3 diesel locomotive - D6546 - which has suddenly appeared from the south on this fine morning. Of course it'll be one of those working a train of cement hoppers from Kent to Scotland but where are they? *SVMRC*.

(*below*) Retford GC shed with the view from the footbridge which conveniently spanned the former main line and the yard of the ex-Manchester Sheffield & Lincolnshire Railway engine shed which had been much rebuilt in recent years. Resident B1 No.61348 appears ready for its next duty. *SVMRC*.

(*above*) Another Mexborough charge, this one being one of the 'Mexborough Pacifics' aka WD Austerity 8F 2-8-0 No.90526 which in true WD style has never been cleaned – painted at works visits but never cleaned – and has even got some extra mess on the front end which looks as though a collision with a lime receptacle has recently taken place. The WD is en route for home with mineral empties which have been brought from Whitemoor yard at March. *SVMRC*.

(*below*) The prototype Deltic sets off for King's Cross after the Retford stop with an afternoon express. The date is during the summer of 1960 long after the big diesel had proved itself and was now earning some revenue for BR. *SVMRC*.

At what speed were they hitting this crossing? It was supposed to be 10 m.p.h. but appearances can be deceptive. Heaton A3 No.60080 DICK TURPIN was about to transfer to Holbeck to take up work on the Settle & Carlisle – with other chosen A3s – but that little expedition was a few weeks off yet on 8th May 1960. No.60080 will probably work as far as Grantham where another A3 would take over for the leg to London. *SVMRC*.

Turning the camera to the south and quickly crossing over to the north side of the flat crossing on that same sunny April afternoon, we see another Tyneside engine heading an express. This is V2 No.60967 from Gateshead which has recently been provided with separate cylinders – November 1958 – and ATC. Having taken on the express at Grantham, the V2 will work the train all the way to Newcastle (Central). Relegated to goods work by the influx of new diesel locomotives, No.60967 transferred to Thornaby in June 1960. *SVMRC*.

In order to make a station stop at Retford, trains off the former MS&LR route bound for Sheffield had to perform a sort of lazy 'S' manoeuvre whereby they came off the route by a spur onto the ECML metals, into the station facing north, and then off again around a long spur which would put them back onto the east-west axis they were following originally. K3 No.61877 has just started its deviation off the MS&L and is about to join the ECML. Such a move saw the train cross – or conflict with – three different routes. The K3 was a newcomer at Lincoln – arrived 20th March 1960 – from where it was working this train. *SVMRC.*

Before it was transferred to Retford on 22nd February 1959, J11 No.64450 had been transferred no less than fifteen times during the forty years since returning from France where she spent two years towards the end of WW1. Retford became its final shed and it enjoyed just over three years there before being condemned on 6th April 1962. A recent shopping had seen the 0-6-0 being fitted with carriage heating apparatus with connections front and rear, a useful asset for a steam locomotive fitted with a vacuum ejector. However, Retford was hardly inundated with passenger train jobs and what they had was easily covered by the depots' B1s. Retford's allocation mainly consisted of freight types 0-6-0s and 2-8-0s and our subject is doing just that in this June 1960 image where No.64450 has charge of a westbound goods and is traversing the flat crossing at a sedate 10 m.p.h. *SVMRC.*

In June 1960, an Up service of the *MASTER CUTLER* gingerly rounds the curve at Retford so as not to alarm any passengers who may be enjoying a drink of tea, coffee or something stronger prior to luncheon service. All signals on the ECML are at danger so it is safe for EE Type D248 to slip onto the Up main and gently tease the engine ready for the dash south once clear of the crossing. *SVMRC.*

Let's have a look at where we have come from prior to venturing onto the ECML. The Pullman has nearly completed the lazy 'S' described earlier. With just six cars on, the train was very easily managed by these 2,000 h.p. monsters and it was easy for them to keep within the timings but they were doing two or three round trips a day from Sheffield (Victoria) to King's Cross. *SVMRC.*

Doing what they were good at, B16/2 No.61475 runs through Retford with a bit of flair – though sticking to the speed limit over the crossing – on an overcast day in 1962. One of York's vast army of B16s, this engine was formerly known as No.61406 but was renumbered on 13th December 1949 to make way for the growing class of Thompson B1s still being delivered. The road is level here but just beyond the station there is a one mile long rise of 1 in 440, which is enough to show some respect hence the maximum speed for the circumstances. No.61475 was transferred to Dairycoates on 13th January 1963 but by mid-April the 4-6-0 was condemned and sent with indecent haste to Darlington for scrapping. *SVMRC*.

Not sure which Pullman this train is but it's a Copley Hill A1 on the point holding back the train for the 10 m.p.h. traverse of the flat crossing. It is 1962 and all pretence at making these locomotives look anything near clean has gone. Luckily carriages could be put through washing plants or they too would have been another factor in BR looking less than impressive to the occasional traveller. No.60141 ABBOTSFORD moved on from 56C to York in September 1963 but was condemned a year later. *SVMRC*.

'It's the one with the funny smoke deflectors!' The older boy is probably trying to impart some knowledge to his younger sibling but such detail didn't really interest these young spotters' as nameplates and 'cops' were more the order of importance to them. A3 No.60061 PRETTY POLLY – there is a name to conjure with – is en route to London stopping at all of the important centres on the way. Note the reversed headboard being returned from whence it came. *SVMRC*.

An express from Leeds (Central) to London (King's Cross) deviates off the main line and heads east towards Lincoln on what could have been a planned Sunday diversion, or an emergency diversion for reasons unknown. The motive power is A4 No.60025 FALCON setting out on what is somewhat unfamiliar territory. We shall be following it shortly! *SVMRC.*

We've heard all the stories about the way King's Cross engine shed kept its engine clean but it wasn't strictly true. Most of those working the principal express trains were kept clean but the others were like the rest of BR's stock carrying a coating of too easily collected filth. There simply were never enough cleaners available, BR didn't attract people like other cleaner industries with better working hours and conditions, especially in the Capital. The external condition of A3 No.60039 SANDWICH – heading a Down express over the flat crossing at Retford – was typical of most BR locomotives in June 1962 just like the unidentified 9F heading south. *SVMRC.*

Peppercorn A1 No.60139 SEA EAGLE runs through Retford with an Up express in July 1962. The pleasing design of Retford South signal box oversees every movement the slightest deviation could cause disaster. Considering the number of conflicting movements using this flat crossing everyday belies the fact that this location was probably one of the safest on BR. *SVMRC.*

To finish off this sequence at Retford, we present this view of Peppercorn A1 No.60125 SCOTTISH UNION, one of Doncaster's own allocation which has stopped at Retford with an Up express in September 1960. The sun is going down but the 'spotters' are still out in force. *SVMRC.*

Lincoln's normal exposure to Pacifics in the latter years of BR was the daily Norwich Thorpe 'Britannia' working the Down and Up services – morning and afternoon – Harwich-Liverpool return (seen earlier) but on certain Sunday's when the ECML was closed at strategic points for upgrading, maintenance, etc., diversions of the Sunday services often brought those ECML expresses and their motive power through Lincoln (Central). Such was the case on this unrecorded Sunday in 1960 when Copley Hill A1 No.60148 ABOYEUR drifted through with what was the Up service of the *HARROGATE SUNDAY PULLMAN*. Note the reversed headboard although some of the carriages are displaying their roof boards. *SVMRC*.

If the spotters' weren't present, the station would be like a graveyard. Typically for the period the bookstall was closed for the sale of Sunday newspapers and everything else! Even though a vast number of the population travelled by train on Sunday the trading laws of the times forbid most outlets of selling goods for gain! Thankfully times have changed at most centres in the UK for the traveller offering better amenities A1 No.60119 PATRICK STIRLING keeps aloft the banner for the 'unclean' and unkempt. *SVMRC*.

Looking south as the Doncaster based Pacific approaches with its Down express. *SVMRC*.

One of 'Top Shed's' A3s – No.60108 GAY CRUSADER – keeps the young spotters' happy. *SVMRC*.

The classic view of the goods yards at New England in July 1960 with one of 34E's two dozen or so BR Standard 9F 2-10-0s departing for the south with a fish train. The vans on the train were about as dirty as the 9F but it didn't appear to matter as all of them would be redundant in six or so years! *SVMRC.*

Having been relieved at Peterborough (North), Doncaster A1 No.60128 BONGRACE proceeds to New England shed for servicing in July 1960. The Pacific had only recently completed a major overhaul and it still looks reasonable. From this vantage point we can see the simplicity of the layout of the former Midland lines compared with the complexity of the Great Northern layout. *SVMRC.*

(*above*) New England also had a raft of these Ivatt Class 4s from new; others were left-overs from the closed sheds on the erstwhile Midland & Great Northern Railway. This is No.43082 with a pair of passenger vehicles heading along the former Midland metals towards Peterborough (East) but from where? It is the summer of 1960 and transition was well underway on BR. This 2-6-0 and her sisters will start to disperse from Peterborough soon but No.43082 remained loyal until November 1963 when it transferred to Barrow Hill; less than two years went by before a move to Langwith Junction took place, however, before that was completed the 4F was condemned in November 1965. Once this two-vehicle formation has been uncoupled at East station, the 2-6-0 would return to 34E for servicing. *SVMRC.*

(*below*) Heading for home Immingham B1 No.61183 departs from the Peterborough (North) stop with a King's Cross-Grimsby express in July 1960. The load appears considerable but the route should not tax the 4-6-0 too much. In the event of having no cleaners available then paint certain items on the front end seems to be the order of the day! If anything the white paint must have highlighted the atrocious filth encasing the locomotive rather than distract. However, even the critics must admit that the scheme appears to have caught on with certain depots adopting paint as the new clean! *SVMRC.*

(*above*) Looking north from the same bridge reveals A1 No.60122 CURLEW approaching whilst a Stanier 8F creeps down from Werrington with a coal train. *SVMRC.*

(*below*) Having come on to this Up express at Grantham, 34A A4 No.60032 GANNET has only just warmed up and has now got to call at Peterborough on this summers' day in 1960. *SVMRC.*

(*above*) Another fitted freight – a long one – sets out from New England yards for the Capital in July 1960. This Doncaster charge has at least got a shed plate but it unfortunately shares the same colour scheme as sister No.92188 and all the other residents of the engine sheds aligning the ECML – various shades of filth. *SVMRC.*

(*below*) Having come off a passenger service it has brought from one of the east coast resorts in the summer of 1959, B17 No.61611 RAYNHAM HALL pulls forward alongside Spital Bridge engine shed to allow Burton based 'Crab' No.42896 to come off shed, and back onto the stock which it would then take to Nottingham, Derby and Burton. This was a regular changeover point for inter-regional passenger workings for both crews and motive power. By October the B17 would be in the works at Doncaster being broken up. *SVMRC.*

A4 No.60023 GOLDEN EAGLE leads a Newcastle express away from Peterborough with minimum effort during the summer of 1960. With twelve on, the A4 has some 192 miles to cover but none of the gradients encountered would be taxing except perhaps the sixteen miles to Stoke summit but even that has nothing more than 1 in 176. The locomotives were built for racing and the ECML is essentially a racetrack – 'horses for courses' as the saying goes! *SVMRC*.

Stanier 8F No.48442 approaches Spital Bridge in July 1960 with an Up freight which surprisingly comprises everything but coal. The 2-8-0 appears to be nearly in ex-works condition, although the first layers of filth are starting to settle nicely on just the horizontal surfaces for now. Note that the 8F has a 16B shed plate which was the first BR shed code issued to Spital Bridge shed but which was changed in 1950 to 35C, then to 31F in 1958! 16B then lay dormant from 1950 to 1955 when Kirkby-in-Ashfield took it on for the next eight years as a promotion from 16C. This 8F was one of the Swindon-built wartime examples and started life at Old Oak Common shed in June 1944 and from there to the LMS and Kirkby-in-Ashfield. No.48442 had four resident periods at Kirkby-in-Ashfield, this latest one starting in the previous April. *SVMRC*.

Fully coaled and watered, Norwich Thorpe B12 No.61572 – it seems strangely familiar that number – runs across the main line en-route from New England motive power depot to Peterborough (East) station to take up a working. Normally engines working into Peterborough from the GE lines would service in the former GER shed behind East station which had closed in 1939 but remained in use for servicing. However, in 1960 a new turntable was installed at the East shed and during the period that the yard was unavailable, engines instead came to New England. *SVMRC*.

Taking the direct route and by-passing North station, No.61572 makes its way south in July 1960. The coal dispensed by the NWE coaling plant leaves a lot to be desired but that too was a sign of the times. Note how busy that footplate is! Finally, there wasn't too many B12s around in 1960 especially those with wrong-facing BR crests on the right side of their tenders! *SVMRC*.

Peppercorn A1 No.60118 ARCHIBALD STURROCK departs for the north with an express from King's Cross whilst a K3 with a Down fitted freight waits for the clear road behind the express. *SVMRC*.

THE LAST YEARS OF STEAM ON THE EASTERN REGION

(*above*) Thick and fast, or so it seemed! Another Down express departs Peterborough on a rather overcast day in 1960. Peppercorn A2 No.60533 HAPPY KNIGHT adds to the overcast with a show of pyrotechnic bliss in the face of all the local smoke abatement laws. Across on the west side of the former Midland line D16 4-4-0s rub shoulders with ex-LMS 4Fs on Spital Bridge shed yard. That shed wasn't too far off closure but right up to the end some three or four of the ex-GER engines resided with a dozen or so 4Fs and twenty other assorted types ranging from 0-6-0Ts to WD 2-8-0s. *SVMRC.*

(*below*) Disgraceful looking A3 No.60111 ENTERPRISE approaches Peterborough (North) with an Up express during the summer of 1960. The Pacific was one of Grantham's steeds. *SVMRC.*

With what appears to be nine passenger bogies in tow, Derby-based 4F No.44169 runs north past the remains of the erstwhile Midland Railway passenger station known as Peterborough Crescent which had opened in 1858 but was closed only eight years later from 1st August 1866! Since that date staff have made use of the building through three changes of ownership; it still seems occupied. It would be interesting to know the origin of this train which by this late summer afternoon was on its way back to the East Midlands. If nothing else, the use of an 0-6-0 on this working shows the capabilities of these 4Fs. *SVMRC*.

Passing Crescent Junction signal box, V2 No.60896 slows for the Peterborough stop with a Down express in July 1960. Shedded at Grantham at this time, the V2 moved to Doncaster in October. It was one of the early V2 casualties being condemned 23rd September 1962. The power station in the background was Peterborough's own which was built in 1951 but which only generated 38 Megawatts at full demand; it was closed by 1985. *SVMRC.*

This image of A4 No.60025 FALCON is included to show the gauge attached to the casing just ahead of the nameplate but was connected to a pipe leading to the lower section of the smokebox. If anyone knows anything about this experiment/trial we would like to hear from you. *SVMRC.*

Just in case you had forgotten what an ordinary A4 looked like when in service. No.60010 DOMINION OF CANADA, with an Up express from the north, arrives at Peterborough (North) in 1959. *SVMRC.*

A fine specimen! With about eleven on, No.60010 departs for London from platform 2. *SVMRC*.

Doncaster's Thompson A2 No.60520 OWEN TUDOR strides out for London over the Nene bridge in July 1960. *SVMRC*.

The enemy was everywhere! It was inevitable that the *SCOTCH GOODS* (1515 King's Cross to Niddrie) fast freight service would go over to diesel haulage shortly after the EE Type 4s were introduced on the ECML if only to see what they could do to sharpen the schedules or even speed up the whole service. This is D207 in the early days – before yellow paint was gradually introduced to the front ends and it was content to stable at Hornsey when in London – of its employment by the Eastern Region negotiating the lines south of Peterborough's Crescent Junction with the fitted freight on a summer evening. How far the big diesel worked is unknown but there is no reason why it didn't work all the way just to prove its versatility and what it was designed to do! *SVMRC.*

EASTERN REGION

Passing through the girders of the Nene bridge Immingham B1 No.61144 takes a *BUTLIN'S EXPRESS* from Skegness back to King's Cross in 1960. The headboard was an ER Press Office idea but the board would have looked much better on a clean locomotive. *SVMRC*.

King's Cross B1 No.61393 runs over the Nene bridge in August 1960 with express headlamps and a trailing load of mainly suburban stock. It must have been 'cross your legs time' for the occupants of those vehicles wherever they were going! Perhaps it was another Butlin's special. The reason why the B1 looks out of the ordinary is down to a recent General overhaul at Doncaster. Peterborough United's London Road football ground is just visible on the left; they still play there nearly sixty years on! *SVMRC*.

(*above*) Time to deviate off the ECML and explore the route to the east via the old Great Eastern metals! Ex-LMS 4F No.43937 is showing us the way as it runs downgrade over the River Nene from Crescent Junction. Behind the last coach is the former MR Nene Junction signal box whilst on the right beneath the power stations coal conveyor is Nene Carriage sidings. *SVMRC.*

(*below*) In July 1960 Rugby based Stanier Class 4 2-6-4T No.42467 brings three ex-LMS coaches forming what appears to be an excursion – W712 – from the Northampton direction which if so would be one of the shortest excursions on record. The route here was historically that of the L&NWR and their erstwhile engine shed named Water End with its northlight roof and which closed in February 1932 can be seen above the train. Since then, this line has been truncated and the engine shed swept away to accommodate the Nene Valley Railway. *SVMRC.*

During the late summer of 1959, Rugby Cl.5 No.44915 heads for home with an afternoon working from Peterborough (East) consisting of a three-coach formation including a Gresley open. In pre-Grouping days this area was the meeting point for the Great Eastern, the Midland, and London & North Western railways. The latter companies each had their own goods warehouses but the station and its environs was pure GER. As we have seen the LNW had their engine shed just to the west of here where the MR line deviates to the north from the LNW line. The MR of course had their roundhouse shed at Spital Bridge. The GE had their engine shed located behind the passenger station to the north-east. The goods yard is quite extensive the interchanging of freight wagons made it necessary before 1948. *SVMRC*.

March based Peppercorn K1 No.62054 sets out for the west with a decent load in 1960. *SVMRC*.

(*above*) Spital Bridge based 4F No.44097 departs from Peterborough (East) with an all stations working to Leicester in 1959. *SVMRC.*

(*below*) Monument Lane Cl.5 No.44842 runs off the Northampton line light engine in June 1960 but showing a special headboard W204. The fact that the engine is working east smokebox first and without any stock begs the question where has the 4-6-0 just originated from; where was it going too; and where would it turn assuming that the East turntable was still out of use, and that it was returning west within the next few hours? Of course No.44842 could easily reverse up to Spital Bridge or even New England sheds to turn once it was clear of the junction here. Now, the eagle-eyed amongst you will have noticed the shed plate which is showing the correct code 21E but in the same manner as written here – in line. *SVMRC.*

above) A Saltley based 4F – No.44333 – hauls a holiday special out of Peterborough (East) in July 1960 and begins to attack the incline up to Crescent Junction. The return route to Birmingham taken by this train would be quite interesting assuming Stamford and Syston Junction are en route. There is plenty of coal for the journey although the quality looks rather dubious! *SVMRC*.

below) Another holiday extra traverses the slope from Crescent Junction in June 1960. The 4F was No.43933 from Kirkby-in-Ashfield with an assortment of stock in tow. Now across the River Nene is the plant which receives the coal for the Peterborough power station. You can see the hordes of 16-ton mineral wagons milling around the building where the wagons were tipped into a bunker which fed the conveyor which then delivered supplies to the generating station on the east side of the ECML. On the embankment below the wagons someone has taken the trouble to inform all and sundry that this place was the CEGB Coaling Plant; they appear to have used pieces of coal to form the figures. *SVMRC*.

Transition! A six-car Metro-Camm DMU, made up of a pair of three car units, runs past the former LNWR engine shed at Water End on a service from Northampton to Peterborough (East) in July 1960. *SVMRC.*

One of New England's WD 2-8-0s, No.90015, puts on a bit of speed to help get its mixed goods up the spur to Crescent Junction from the GEF line. The lofty signal box at East station can be seen above the parapet of the London Road bridge. *SVMRC.*

(*above*) The proximity of the railway cottages to the East station throat must be one of the closest on BR. That washing didn't really stand much of a chance although Ivatt Cl.4 No.43094 is keeping the smoke down. *SVMRC*.

(*berlow*) J6 No.64177 brings a mixed freight consisting mainly brick wagons into Peterborough East in June 1960. *SVMRC*.

Parkeston B1 No.61372 comes off a train it has just brought from the East coast into Peterborough (East). The 4-6-0 is drawing forward to clear the points whilst the new train engine is nowhere to be seen at this moment in time having gone beyond the bridge; yes it was the Ivatt No.43094 from Kings Lynn, which would be something of a rarity west of Peterborough. The signal box straddling the platform line is Peterborough East which in April 1932 replaced Fletton Road signal box located just a little to the west. *SVMRC.*

(*above*) March B17 No.61626 BRANCEPETH CASTLE comes off the train it has just arrived with at East station in June 1959. The 4-6-0 would transfer to Cambridge on 6th December next but five weeks later whilst attending Doncaster shops it was condemned and then broken up. *SVMRC*.

(*below*) Norwich Thorpe shed was represented by D16 No.62511 which was striding out for the west with a lightweight load in June 1959. *SVMRC*.

(*above*) When the 'Britannia's were King on the Great Eastern Line expresses! Cambridge engine shed with Norwich Thorpe 'Britannia' No.70006 ROBERT BURNS stabled awaiting its next duty. If there was one place where this class made an impact it was on the former Great Eastern main line expresses which were transformed overnight into serious express workings. The GE enginemen took to them, revelled in them and hammered them. *SVMRC*.

(*below*) Cambridge shed with the more usual fare hogging its stabling roads in July 1959. Boston based Ivatt Cl.4 No.43107 looks quite Americanised compared with the smooth lines of the resident B1. *SVMRC*.

Thompson O1 No.63803 from March threads its way out of Cambridge yard and heads for home with a train of vans during the summer of 1959. March was the only shed on the former GE Lines which had an allocation of these fine 2-8-0s which would have become the LNER standard had Thompson remained in the job and the LNER lasted perhaps ten years longer. As it was they had short lives being victims of the onward progress of modernisation. *SVMRC.*

At the other end of Cambridge station B17 No.61620 CLUMBER was heading south with an Up express. *SVMRC.*

This is Colchester in November 1958 with overhead catenary, a shed built to house diesel locomotives, and this ancient J15 0-6-0 No.65445 working a three-coach set in spite of all the electric and diesel services. The J15 was still allocated to Colchester at the time – it had spent twenty-seven years of its life here – and had not been in works for at least six months but maintenance caught up with it and during the summer of 1962 it was condemned and cut up at Stratford. *SVMRC.*

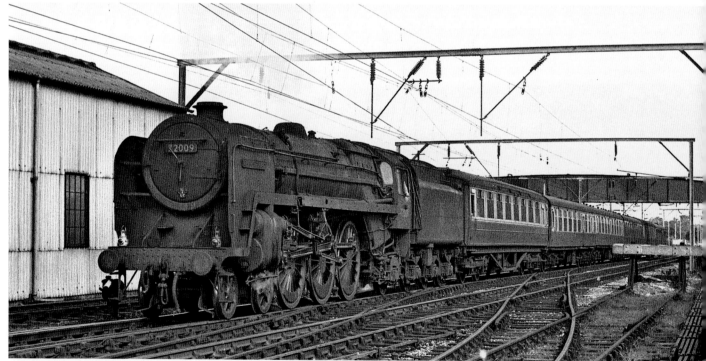

Just when you thought it was safe to get the diesel book out along comes another steam locomotive but not any old steamer, this was BR Standard 'Clan' Pacific No.72009 CLAN STEWART which was on loan from Carlisle Kingmoor for evaluation trials at Stratford from September to December 1958. Between the lines the evaluation read - 'What can we do with these locomotives surplus to our requirements perhaps you could use them?' But the GE lines had the EE Type 4s on their way however in the meantime all those 'Brits' would be just fine and they were clean! *SVMRC.*

(*above*) Back on the ECML now and it's a straight run into King's Cross with no more deviations, west or east! Just eighteen miles to the bufferstops at the terminus although this train will not be going that far; Hornsey would be a safe bet! It's a fairly quiet moment at Hatfield as New England WD 2-8-0 No.90659 drifts past the Up platform – and the intending passengers – after taking refuge in one of the Up side sidings whilst an express or two ran past. The freight is a bit of a mixed bag with small – industrial – coal and other items, and the trains weight would hardly tax the WD even with an adverse 1 in 200 gradient waiting just beyond the station and that tender full of coal dust and other rubbish. The date is at some time during the summer of 1959 more than a year after that 35A shedplate should have been removed in favour of the 34E code which replaced it. *SVMRC*.

(*below*) As No.90659 gets underway an approaching Cambridge service prepares for its Hatfield stop. The motive power is D5318 one of the recently acquired BRC&W Type 2 diesel-electric locomotives which were replacing B17s and B2s on jobs such as this. In the distance a Cravens DMU also approaches from the south. *SVMRC*.

The Type 2 has arrived in Down platform No.2 and the DMU has also arrived at the other Down platform face No.3 with an all-stations to Hitchin. Then, just as they stop along comes an express on the Up main with A4 No.60025 FALCON in charge and running nicely with little exhaust, plenty of steam and a chime on the whistle for the photographer; we are back in seventh heaven! Now then, I mentioned earlier that it was quiet and in a few minutes it will be again but for now it's rather busy except for the intending passengers on platform 1 who must now be wondering when their train will show-up! *SVMRC*.

And here it comes! B1 No.61207 another of New England's charges with a semi-fast to King's Cross. The train consisted of some interesting articulated units and six-wheel vans; I wonder what that ride was like? The B1 which spent the whole of its life working from New England has the correct 34E shedplate. *SVMRC.*

We like WD 2-8-0s! No.90730 with a train of bricks and coal takes the Up fast as a 350 h.p. 0-6-0DE shunter propels a stores train into the Up platform. *SVMRC.*

No stopping! King's Cross V2 No.60914 has eleven on and is preparing for the change in gradient as it leaves Hatfield behind for the climb to Welwyn Garden City with a Down express during that summer of 1959. *SVMRC.*

'Anyway, I put the bet on...' Seemingly oblivious to the passing express but obviously not, two linemen walk along the Up fast as A1 No.60136 ALCAZAR from Doncaster rips past them with a Down service. Note the position of the 36A shed plate – different or what? *SVMRC.*

A3 No.60063 ISINGLASS sweeps beneath the bridge north of the station which overlooks the Up goods yard and carriage siding. In the background is the Red Lion Hotel, one of the few hostelries in Hatfield. *SVMRC.*

What are we burning here? V2 No.60983 hurries through Hatfield with a Down express before the Smoke Inspectors get wind of its passage. Alongside the station N7 No.69629 – working a coal train of just eight wagons – was also contributing to the smoke screen. *SVMRC.*

B17 No.61652 DARLINGTON with a train consisting two Quad-Art sets. The date is sometime during the summer of 1959 and No.61652 had spent the last nine years working from Cambridge shed, mainly on the passenger services to King's Cross. By now, the 4-6-0 was just days away from being condemned, a deed carried out when it entered the works at Doncaster on 17th September. *SVMRC*.

With just nine bogies on, QUICKSILVER impressing the locals at Hatfield as she rushes through with the Down service of *THE TALISMAN* in 1961. *SVMRC*.

(*above*) Another Immingham B1 working Grimsby's express passenger link with the Capital! Not quite up to 34A's standard of cleaning but Immingham was never known for turning out express passenger engines per hour! No.61143 had two more bogies in tow than No.60015 but she had only half the distance to travel and nearly the same amount of time to do so. *SVMRC*.

(*below*) Yet another northbound express with immaculate A4 No.60029 WOODCOCK in charge of twelve bogies! Look no exhaust but the train was on the level here and going fast. *SVMRC*.

Are we there yet!? We've reached the outer suburbs of the Capital now and as a result of the Widening from two tracks to four completed in 1959, traffic into and out of King's Cross was flowing much easier. Friday afternoon and evening in particular used to be hectic times with expresses queuing with suburban trains to get through the bottleneck tunnels at Hadley Wood North and South along with this much longer bore at Potters Bar. A4 No.60008 DWIGHT D. EISENHOWER is traversing the Down fast on Friday 31st May 1963 with a northbound express. *PL/BLP*.

The gradient here is against the Down trains – 1 in 200 for nearly nine miles from Hornsey – but the LNER equipped the ECML with locomotives which could cope with the hills and the heavy loads. On 31st May 1963 V2 No.60982 was far from working hard as it rattled along with a Newcastle-Kings Cross express before plunging into the 1214 yard Potters Bar bore. The original tunnel was now taking both of the Up lines whereas the new tunnels on the right here, took the re-arranged Down lines. Just over twelve miles out and its downhill all the way or should that be Up! *PL/BLP*.

The Down *ANGLO-SCOTTISH CAR CARRIER* skirts through the cutting at Potters Bar before encountering the tunnel. This train was one of BR's more successful ventures and its introduction spawned other services which ran north and south, east and west, and even had some sleeper trains too. The motive power for this service is Doncaster A1 No.60128 BONGRACE (see also page 85 – it seems they did clean them). *PL/BLP*.

On a date to be defined, but post Widening and looking like summer 1960, L1 No.67746 in charge of two sets of Quad-Arts takes the Up fast through Potters Bar. The Thompson 2-6-4T was allocated to Hitchin from 2nd January 1949 until 18th September 1960 when it went to 34A for five and a half months prior to transferring to Colwick. *SVMRC*.

A1 SEA EAGLE clears Potters Bar tunnel with a Down express at the height of summer in 1961. *SVMRC.*

A different view of GREEN ARROW! Heading north through Potters Bar in 1961. *SVMRC.*

(*opposite, top*) We are now at Hadley Wood – about eleven miles from the terminus – and we encounter this Up fitted freight with Monument Lane's Stanier Cl.5 No.45180 which was rather off its normal route on 17th May 1963. How the 4-6-0 got onto the ECML is unknown but the two ex-LMS conduits feeding Peterborough from the west seem the most likely answer. (*opposite, centre*) Between the tunnels! This may well be the 1515 King's Cross-Niddrie goods with Doncaster A1 No.60128 BONGRACE looking anything but on Friday 17th May 1963. (*opposite*) The difference is in the finish! On the same afternoon, nicely turned out, A4 No.60025 is well into its stride as its exits Hadley Wood south tunnel with a Down express. *All PL/BLP.*

The ECML at its southern end especially, with two Up and two Down lines, was busy for most of the time with interludes when more than one train might be passing the observer or photographer. During the late afternoon of 16th March 1963 Paul Leavens recorded some of the hectic activity of northbound expresses leaving the Capital as the Up trains were arriving. The motive power was quite varied as witnesses the following four pages: 9F No.92145 heads along the slow line with a Down freight consisting empty brick wagons going back to Peterborough. *PL/BLP*.

Now why would anyone want to insert a van in the middle of a mineral train? New England WD 8F No.90659 – again – drifts down the 1 in 200 away from the tunnel with a loaded coal train. *PL/BLP*.

No sooner was the WD drawing level with the photographer than A1 No.60130 KESTREL came thundering out of the twin-bore tunnel with a very smart looking express made up entirely of new Mk.1 coaches. The Copley Hill Pacific herself was looking rather nice too having been ex-works for less than a month. *PL/BLP*.

A brisk walk south now along the P-Way! We have got to a point where the flyover for the Hertford line swings over the ECML in a north-easterly direction. Another southbound freight came past, again WD hauled and mixed but mainly containing mineral wagons. No.90130 was the 2-8-0 involved – you'll have to take our word for that – and it was shedded at where else but New England. Just a month after running this freight into London the 'Austerity' transferred to Retford and then two years later to Colwick. *PL/BLP*.

Not sure of the destination of this Down express but the Thompson A2/3 No.60520 OWEN TUDOR – again – was a New England engine and the livery sort of gives you a clue. So, Peterborough may well have been the objective, initially. *PL/BLP.*

Our first BR-built diesel locomotive sneaked on to the page when this V2 – No.60948 – was bringing a train of cement empties out of the tunnel. The Sulzer Type 4 – D148 – has charge of nine Pullman cars which may have been the *TEES-TYNE PULLMAN. PL/BLP.*

As the day wore on the sun moved round to the west and then started its inevitable fall towards the horizon. Shadows were growing longer but the traffic kept coming. This is Doncaster V2 No.60899 on the Down slow with a very mixed fitted freight passing Down Box Wood Green Tunnel.

It is now 30th May 1963 and we are at the south portal of the 705 yards long Wood Green tunnel as V2 No.60950 heads north with an express. It is interesting to note that every compartment window and the drop windows on the doors including Guards own compartment were open. Admitted there was no air conditioning then, and it was a warm evening but the perils of the smoke and dirt – look at those windows – from the locomotive appeared more inviting than the heat. The fairly new Mk.1 coach has the legend EAST COAST on the end panel. *PL/BLP*.

(*above*) Only to be expected, a filthy A3 – No.60108 GAY CRUSADER again this time but with smoke deflectors – has charge of a Down express and is running well as it exits the north portal of Wood Green tunnel on the evening of 11th June 1963. Now back to our southerly jaunt towards KX. *PL/BLP*.

(*below*) We've seen the diesel-hauled service earlier but this steam hauled occasion must have come about as a result of the diesel/diesels failing north of here. This is BR Standard 9F No.92149 working the Uddingston-Cliffe empties of the service back to Kent. Bathed by the evening sun as it runs through New Southgate on 11th June 1963, the New England based 2-10-0 is running late but at least it is running. At what stage the 9F would leave the train is unknown – would it work through to SR metals or leave the train in one of the ER London yards for the SR to retrieve? This daily operation could soon become undone in the event of a failure. By the end of June steam would be effectively banned on the ECML south of Peterborough but incidents such as this would bring steam back to the Capital time and time again. For such instances, the turntable at Hornsey was left in situ for a few years. *PL/BLP*.

A4 No.60017 SILVER FOX was a regular on the *ANGLO-SCOTTISH CAR CARRIER* and on the 11th June 1963 she runs the Up service over the final few miles through New Southgate. *PL/BLP*.

The A4s were making a good show of it towards the end in London: No.60006 SIR RALPH WEDGWOOD accelerates through Holloway Road with a Down express on the morning of Monday 10th June 1963. *PL/BLP*.

(*above*) Just days before operations concerning steam locomotives are wound up at King's Cross shed, three northbound trains battle the 1 in 107 gradient through Holloway on Friday 14th June 1963. *All PL/BLP*.

THE LAST YEARS OF STEAM ON THE EASTERN REGION

(*above*) Its work done on the main line, A4 No.60017 SILVER FOX is uncoupled from an Up service of the *ANGLO-SCOTTISH CAR CARRIER* at Holloway on Friday evening 14th June 1963. Holloway was the terminus for this train, the road vehicles being unloaded at a special facility created for the daily but seasonal trains. The A4 would retire to 'Top Shed' whilst other motive power would take care of the train. Note the corridor tender which shows a remarkably small amount of coal usage which indicates that No.60017 joined this train at Peterborough. The service became very popular with the public and the terminal itself – with basic amenities being just that – was subject to a question in Parliament on 15th December 1965 when Lord Ferrier asked Her Majesty's Government to urge BR to improve conditions for passengers awaiting the unloading of their vehicles by providing seats and/or shelter, and other facilities. The noble Lord was quietly told to go and ask the BR Board himself...! *Both PL/BLP.*

We move onto 34A shed now to see what was afoot and the first thing we see is this little group. They still had it! Nos.60007 SIR NIGEL GRESLEY; 60017 SILVER FOX; and 60044 MELTON; at 'Top Shed' on 23rd March 1963. *PL/BLP.*

(*above*) Regular visitors to King's Cross, the WD 2-8-0s from New England use to lower the tone of the place with their permanent filth plastered exteriors but of late they were joined by many of 34As own allocation and therefore blended as though they were not there. This is No.90158 in the company of 9F 2-10-0s on Sunday 26th May 1963. *PL/BLP*.

(*below*) A once proud line-up at King's Cross shed but on 26th May 1963 they were all looking rather tired: No.60158 ABERDONIAN, 60112 ST. SIMON, and 60029 WOODCOCK. *PL/BLP*.

above) Having been summoned to work a special from King's cross on 9th June 1963, Princess Coronation No.46245 CITY OF LONDON moves off the 'Bottom Shed' locomotive yard on Saturday 8th June to try the relevant platforms and crossings prior to the special working on the Sunday morning. The 'Duchess' looks nice and smart as would be expected for such a duty which on the day was a special to Doncaster locomotive works and return for the Home Counties Railway Society. *PL/BLP*.

below) A3 No.60107 ROYAL LANCER complete with smoke deflectors, sets off from King's Cross on 11th June 1963. *PL/BLP*.

No.60107 departs King's Cross in August 1960, its train looking far from full. Probably only going as far as Grantham, the A1's tender is not exactly overflowing with coal but there is plenty for a Grantham job. *SVMRC*.

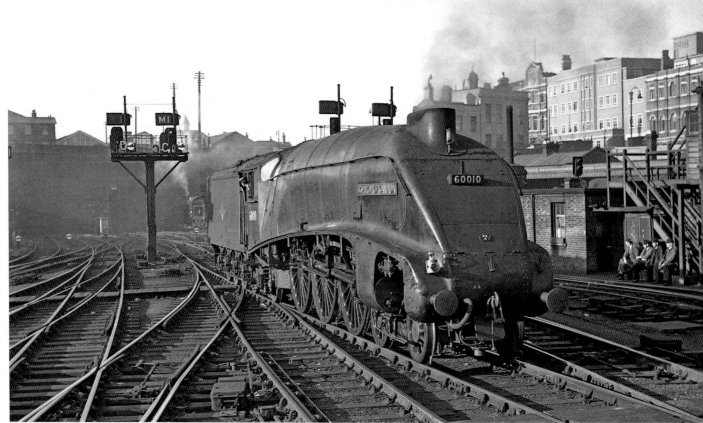

Its work for the day being completed, A4 No.60010 DOMINION OF CANADA reverses out of King's Cross terminus en route to 'Top Shed' on an August evening in 1960. We have reached the end! *SVMRC*.